Igor I. Sikorsky, Jr.

AA'S GODPARENTS

Three Early Influences on Alcoholics Anonymous and Its Foundation

CARL JUNG

EMMET FOX

JACK ALEXANDER

CompCare® Publishers
2415 Annapolis Lane
Minneapolis, Minnesota 55441

Published in the United States
by CompCare Publishers.

Sikorsky, Igor I., 1929-
AA's godparents: three early influences on Alcoholics Anonymous and its foundation, Carl Jung, Emmet Fox, Jack Alexander / Igor I. Sikorsky, Jr.
p. 54 cm.
ISBN 0-89638-199-4: $3.95
1. Alcoholics Anonymous—History. 2. Alcoholics—Rehabilitation—History—20th century. 3. Jung, C.G. (Carl Gustav), 1875-1961. 4. Fox, Emmet. 5. Alexander, Jack, d. 1975. I. Title.
HV5278.S55 1990 362.29′286—dc20 89-25341
CIP

Cover and interior design by Lillian Svec

Inquiries, orders, and catalog requests should be addressed to
CompCare Publishers
2415 Annapolis Lane
Minneapolis, Minnesota 55441
Call toll free 800/328-3330
(Minnesota residents 612/559-4800)

5 4 3 2 1
94 93 92 91 90

CONTENTS

INTRODUCTION

All Men of Faith Have Courage

At a crucial time in the development of Alcoholics Anonymous there appeared individuals who were not alcoholics but whose inspiration and interest in the growing fellowship infused it with strength and a spiritual direction. Three of these individuals are described in the following pages.

Carl Jung, the distinguished psychiatrist, was, in the words of Bill Wilson, owed a "long overdue message of deep appreciation" for his role in founding the fellowship, which is best summarized in the classic exchange of correspondence between Bill W. and Carl Jung.

Emmet Fox was a distinguished theologian and religious lecturer in the 1930s and 1940s. Before there was any official AA literature, his work served as the basic text for recovering alcoholics. Part 2 of this book contains a brief outline of Emmet Fox's life and his role in AA.

Part 3 contains the famous Jack Alexander article, "Alcoholics Anonymous," that appeared in the *Saturday Evening Post* in 1941. According to AA's *Grapevine,* that article marked a "milestone in the history of this fellowship." At the time of that report—March 1941—AA had two thousand members; the article inspired a deluge of mail and was a key factor in the explosive growth of AA in the 1940s.

A godparent is defined as one who, while not a direct biological parent, serves to infuse the spiritual life of the child; in this manner, Jung, Fox, and Alexander served as godparents of AA's spiritual foundation.

Basic to the Big Book's recital of the origin of Alcoholics Anonymous is the recognition that "God had done for [us] what [we] could not do for ourselves." Bill's story (found on page 11 of the Big Book) recounts a sober alcoholic visiting him in the depths of a hangover and attributing sobriety to belief in a Higher Power. At that point, Bill felt "floored," and it began to dawn on him "as though religious people were right after all." The miracle of faith came to Bill not through theology but through the miracle of a sober alcoholic whose very presence and sobriety "shouted great tidings."

These ideas were not discovered anew by Bill W. but were part of a tradition as old as man. However, in the field of alcoholism it was Dr. William D. Silkworth—the New York alcoholism specialist considered a medical saint by AA members—who believed that the alcoholic's only hope for recovery lay in "a moral inventory, confession of personality defects, restitution to those harmed, helpfulness to others, and the necessity of belief and dependence upon God."

Thus from the earliest time AA taught the necessity of relying upon "a power greater than ourselves." AA was based on (1) a reliance upon a Higher Power; (2) a thorough and fearless moral housecleaning; and (3) the necessity of carrying this message to other alcoholics. On these three foundations AA was built and maintained, and its membership multiplied. The founders of AA stated:

> The great fact is just this, and nothing less: That we have had deep and effective spiritual experiences which have revolutionized our whole attitude toward life, toward our fellows, and toward God's universe. The central fact of our lives today is the absolute certainty that our Creator has entered into our hearts and

> lives in a way which is indeed miraculous. He has commenced to accomplish those things for us which we could never do by ourselves.
>
> If you are as seriously alcoholic as we were, we believe there is no middle-of-the-road solution. We were in a position where life was becoming impossible, and if we had passed into the region from which there is no return through human aid, we had but two alternatives: One was to go on to the bitter end, blotting out the consciousness of our intolerable situation as best we could, and the other, to accept spiritual help.

With a compulsion stronger than anything else within them, alcoholics at certain times have no mental defense against taking the first drink. Experience demonstrates that they can't think or will themselves to sobriety. The alcoholic's defense must come from a Higher Power.

Elsewhere in the Big Book the emphasis on that crucial foundation is repeated. "Whether the family goes on a spiritual basis or not, the alcoholic member has to if he would recover" (Big Book, page 135). In describing a Twelve Step call, the Big Book states (page 155): "When our friend related his experience, the man agreed that no amount of will power he might muster could stop his drinking for long. A spiritual experience, he conceded, was absolutely necessary, but the price seemed high upon the basis suggested." Incidentally, this encounter describes the historic first meeting of Bill W. and Dr. Bob, AA's co-founders.

When a sick and suffering alcoholic looks at a member of AA with skepticism, AA responds:

> We know what you are thinking. You are saying to yourself: "I'm jittery and alone. I couldn't do

> that." But you can. You forget that you have just now tapped a source of power much greater than yourself. To duplicate, with such backing, what we have accomplished is only a matter of willingness, patience, and labor.... Still you may say: "But I will not have the benefit of contact with you who write this book." We cannot be sure. God will determine that, so you must remember that your real reliance is always upon Him. He will show you how to create the fellowship you crave.
>
> Our book is meant to be suggestive only. We realize we know only a little. God will constantly disclose more to you and to us. Ask Him in your morning meditation what you can do each day for the man who is still sick. The answers will come, if your own house is in order. But obviously you cannot transmit something you haven't got. See to it that your relationship with Him is right, and great events will come to pass for you and countless others. This is the Great Fact for us.
>
> Abandon yourself to God as you understand God. Admit your faults to Him and to your fellows. Clear away the wreckage of your past. Give freely of what you find and join us. We shall be with you in the Fellowship of the Spirit, and you will surely meet some of us as you trudge the Road of Happy Destiny. (Big Book, pages 163-164)

At the time the first edition of the Big Book was written, of the original group that made up Alcoholics Anonymous, over 50 percent were atheists or agnostics. But when they abandoned themselves to God, *as they understood Him*, and followed the action steps of the fellowship, the Twelfth Step promised a spiritual awakening. In conclusion the founders of AA stated:

> We never apologize for anyone for depending upon our Creator. We can laugh at those who think spirituality the way of weakness. Paradoxically, it is the way of strength . . . all men of faith have courage. They trust their God. We never apologize for God. Instead we let Him demonstrate, through us, what He can do. We ask Him to remove our fear and direct our attention to what He would have us be. At once, we commence to outgrow fear. (page 68)

Part One

The Carl Jung-Bill Wilson Connection

For AA members, the name of Carl Jung has long had a special significance, as one of those nonalcoholics who appeared coincidentally at a crucial point during the early movement to inject a particular wisdom. Jung made the greatest strides of our century in treating the loss of meaning in man's life and in recognizing it as a spiritual illness. He criticized the assumption that man is a self-contained, rational creature in a fixed space-time box that measures all reality. He came to the conclusion that destructive emotional states can be healed only as one is brought into contact with a transpersonal reality, by one who has experienced the same travail: "Only the wounded physician can heal."

Jung was consulted by people from all over the world. Jung's important contribution is summarized in the following words, which have been more widely quoted than any others ever written by him:

> Among all my patients in the second half of life—that is to say, over thirty-five—there has not been one whose problem in the last resort was not that of finding a religious outlook on life. It is safe to say that every one of them fell ill because he had lost that which the living religions of every age have given to their followers, and none of them has been really healed who did not regain his religious outlook. (*Modern Man in Search of a Soul,* page 229)

Jung saw that the healing of mind and body could not be accomplished without healing the soul; the journey into the unconscious led past the ego to the seat of healing and growth—the psyche. This is significant, for it flew in the face of the prevailing medical theory of rational personality. According to early theory, evil or bad actions were the functions of the will—and could, therefore, be punished. Alcoholism was labeled a "personality disorder attributable to lack of will." So it was believed that alcoholics could change only if subjected to enough pressures or harsh disapproval.

Early in AA history, Bill W. wrote "a long overdue letter of great appreciation" to Jung as follows:

> May I first introduce myself as Bill W., a co-founder of the Society of Alcoholics Anonymous. Though you have surely heard of us, I doubt if you are aware that a certain conversation you once had with one of your patients, a Mr. Roland H., back in the early 1930s did play a critical role in the founding of our Fellowship.
>
> Though Roland H. has long since passed away, the recollection of his remarkable experience while under treatment by you has definitely become part of AA history. Our remembrance of Roland H.'s statements about his experience with you is as follows:
>
> Having exhausted other means of recovery from his alcoholism, it was about 1931 that he became your patient. I believe he remained under your care for perhaps a year. His admiration for you was boundless, and he left you with a feeling of much confidence.
>
> To his great consternation, he soon relapsed into intoxication. Certain that you were his "court of last resort," he again returned to your care. Then followed the conversation between you that was to become the first link in the

chain of events that led to the founding of Alcoholics Anonymous.

My recollection of his account of that conversation is this: First of all, you frankly told him of his hopelessness, so far as any further medical or psychiatric treatment might be concerned. This candid and humble statement of yours was beyond doubt the first foundation stone upon which our Society has since been built.

Coming from you, one he so trusted and admired, the impact upon him was immense.

When he then asked you if there was any other hope, you told him that there might be, provided he could become the subject of a spiritual or religious experience—in short, a genuine conversion. You pointed out how such an experience, if brought about, might remotivate him when nothing else could. But you did caution, though, that while such experiences had sometimes brought recovery to alcoholics, they were, nevertheless, comparatively rare. You recommended that he place himself in a religious atmosphere and hope for the best. This I believe was the substance of your advice.

Shortly thereafter, Mr. H. joined the Oxford Group, an evangelical movement then at the height of its success in Europe, and one with which you are doubtless familiar. You will remember their large emphasis upon the principles of self-survey, confession, restitution, and giving of oneself in service to others. They strongly stressed meditation and prayer. In these surroundings, Roland H. did find a conversion experience that released him for the time being from his compulsion to drink.

Returning to New York, he became very active with the "O.G." here, then led by an Episcopal clergyman, Dr. Samuel Shoemaker. Dr. Shoemaker had been one of the founders of that movement, and his was a powerful personality that carried immense sincerity and conviction.

At this time (1932-34), the Oxford Group had already sobered a number of alcoholics, and Roland, feeling that he could especially identify with these sufferers, addressed himself to the help of still others. One of these chanced to be an old schoolmate of mine, named Edwin T. ("Ebby"). He had been threatened with commitment to an institution, but Mr. H. and another ex-alcoholic "O.G." member procured his parole, and helped to bring about his sobriety.

Meanwhile, I had run the course of alcoholism and was threatened with commitment myself. Fortunately, I had fallen under the care of a physician—a Dr. William D. Silkworth—who was wonderfully capable of understanding alcoholics. But just as you had given up on Roland, so had he given me up. It was his theory that alcoholism had two components—an obsession that compelled the sufferer to drink against his will and interest, and some sort of metabolism difficulty which he then called an allergy. The alcoholic's compulsion guaranteed that the alcoholic's drinking would go on, and the allergy made sure that the sufferer would finally deteriorate, go insane, or die. Though I had been one of the few he had thought it possible to help, he was finally obliged to tell me of my hopelessness; I, too, would have to be locked up. To me, this was a shattering blow. Just as Roland had been made ready for his conversion experience by you, so had my wonderful friend Dr. Silkworth prepared me.

Hearing of my plight, my friend Edwin T. came to see me at my home, where I was drinking. By then, it was November 1934. I had long marked my friend Edwin for a hopeless case. Yet here he was in a very evident state of "release," which could by no means be accounted for by his mere association for a very short time with the Oxford Group. Yet this obvious state of release, as distinguished from the usual depression, was tremendously convincing. Because he was a kindred sufferer, he could unquestionably communicate with me at great depth. I knew at once I must find an experience like his, or die.

Again I returned to Dr. Silkworth's care, where I could be once more sobered and so gain a clearer view of my friend's experience of release, and of Roland H.'s approach to him.

Clear once more of alcohol, I found myself terribly depressed. This seemed to be caused by my inability to gain the slightest faith. Edwin T. again visited me and repeated the simple Oxford Group formulas. Soon after he left me, I became even more depressed. In utter depair, I cried out, "If there be a God, will He show Himself." There immediately came to me an illumination of enormous impact and dimension, something which I have since tried to describe in the book *Alcoholics Anonymous* and also in *AA Comes of Age,* basic texts which I am sending to you.

My release from the alcohol obsession was immediate. At once, I knew I was a free man.

Shortly following my experience, my friend Edwin came to the hospital, bringing me a copy of William James's *Varieties of Religious Experience.* This book gave me the realization that most conversion experiences, whatever their variety, do have a common denominator of ego collapse at depth. The individual faces an impossible dilemma. In my case, the dilemma had been created by my compulsive drinking, and the deep feeling of hopelessness had been vastly deepened by my doctor. It was deepened still more by my alcoholic friend when he acquainted me with your verdict of hopelessness respecting Roland H.

In the wake of my spiritual experience, there came a vision of a society of alcoholics, each identifying with and transmitting his experience to the next—chain-style. If each sufferer were to carry the news of the scientific hopelessness of alcoholism to each new prospect, he might be able to lay every newcomer wide open to a transforming spiritual experience. This concept proved to be the foundation of such success as Alcoholics Anonymous has since achieved. This has made conversion experiences—nearly every variety reported by James—available on almost a wholesale basis.

So to you, to Dr. Shoemaker of the Oxford Group, to William James, and to my own physician, Dr. Silkworth, we of AA owe this tremendous benefaction. As you will now clearly see, this astonishing chain of events actually started long ago in your consulting room, and it was directly founded upon your own humility and deep perception.

Very many thoughtful AAs are students of your writings. Because of your conviction that man is something more than intellect, emotion, and two dollars' worth of chemicals, you have especially endeared yourself to us. . . .

You will also be interested to learn that, in addition to the "spiritual experience," many AAs report a great variety of psychic phenomena, the cumulative weight of which is very considerable. Other members have—following their recovery in AA—been much helped by your practitioners. A few have been intrigued by the *I Ching* and your remarkable introduction to that work.

Please be certain that your place in the affection, and in the history, of our Fellowship is like no other.

Gratefully yours

January 30, 1961

Carl Jung's response follows:

Your letter has been very welcome indeed.

I had no news from Roland H. anymore and often wondered what has been his fate. Our conversation which he has adequately reported to you had an aspect of which he did not know. The reason that I could not tell him everything was that in those days I had to be exceedingly careful of what I said. I had found out that I was misunderstood in every possible way. Thus I was very careful when I talked to Roland H.

But what I really thought about was the result of many experiences with men of his kind.

His craving for alcohol was the equivalent, on a low level, of the spiritual thirst of our being for wholeness, expressed in medieval language: the union with God.*

How could one formulate such an insight in a language that is not misunderstood in our days?

The only right and legitimate way to such an experience is that it happens to you in reality, and it can only happen to you when you walk on a path which leads you to higher understanding. You might be led to that goal by an act of grace or through a personal and honest contact with friends, or through a higher education of the mind beyond the confines of mere rationalism. I see from your letter that Roland H. has chosen the second way, which was, under the circumstances, obviously the best one.

I am strongly convinced that the evil principle prevailing in this world leads the unrecognized spiritual need into perdition if it is not counteracted either by real religious insight or by the protective wall of human community. An ordinary man, not protected by an action from above and isolated in society, cannot resist the power of evil, which is called very aptly the Devil. But the use of such words arouses so many mistakes that one can only keep aloof from them as much as possible.

These are the reasons why I could not give a full and sufficient explanation to Roland H., but I am risking it with you because I conclude from your very decent and honest letter that you have acquired a point of view above the misleading platitudes one usually hears about alcoholism.

You see, "alcohol" in Latin is *spiritus*, and you use the same word for the highest religious experience as well as for the most depraving poison. The helpful formula therefore is: *spiritus contra spiritum.*

Thanking you again for your kind letter.

Bill's reply to Dr. Jung's letter was dated March 20, 1961. It reads, in part:

Your observation that drinking motivations often include that of a quest for spiritual values caught our special interest. I am sure that, on reflection, thousands of our members could testify that this had been true of them, despite the fact that they often drank for oblivion, for grandiosity, and for other undesirable motives. Sometimes, it seems unfortunate that alcohol, used in excess, turns out to be a deformer of consciousness, as well as an addictive poison.

Years ago, some of us read with great benefit your book entitled *Modern Man in Search of a Soul.* You observed, in effect, that most persons having arrived at age forty and having acquired no conclusions or faith as to who they were, or where they were, or where they were going next in the cosmos, would be bound to encounter increasing neurotic difficulties; and that this would be likely to occur whether their youthful aspirations for sex union, security, and a satisfactory place in society had been satisfied or not. In short, they could not continue to fly blind toward no destination at all, in a universe seemingly having little purpose or meaning. Neither could any amount of resolution, philosophical speculation, or superficial religious conditioning save them from the dilemma in which they found themselves. So long as they lacked any direct spiritual awakening and therefore awareness, their conflict simply had to increase.

These views of yours, doctor, had an immense impact upon some of the early members of our AA Fellowship. We saw that you had perfectly described the impasse in which we had once been, but from which we had been delivered through our several spiritual awakenings. This "spiritual experience" had to be our key to survival and growth. We saw that the alcoholic's helplessness could be turned to vital advantage. By the admission of this, he could be deflated at depth, thus fulfilling the first condition of a remotivating conversion experience.

So the foregoing is still another example of your great helpfulness to us of AA in our formative period. Your words really carried authority, because you seemed to be neither wholly a theologian nor a pure scientist. Therefore, you seemed to stand with us in that no-man's-land that lies between the two—the very place that many of us had found ourselves. Your identification with us was therefore deep and convincing. You spoke a language of the heart that we could understand.

There was no reply to Bill's second letter. Two months later, on June 6, 1961, Dr. Jung died. Bill, having waited a quarter of a century to write his thank-you note, had sent it just in time.

This extraordinary exchange of letters at the twilight of both their lives revealed not only the direct historical influence of Carl Jung on the Alcoholics Anonymous movement but is also the development of Jung's theory—postulated in all his writings, but particularly vividly in his *Answer to Job*—of a duality between the forces of good and evil. The correspondence also was an example of the immense influence that Jung had with so many groups. AA now has a membership of many millions and has indirectly affected countless others. Small group associations in which the "wounded physician" shared in an atmosphere of honesty his own path of recovery were followed by Gamblers Anonymous, Narcotics Anonymous, Emotions Anonymous, Weight Watchers, Overeaters Anonymous, Al-Anon, Alateen and Adult Children of Alcoholics. All these groups owe "a long overdue message of deep appreciation" for the role Carl Jung played in their foundation, for his search for the religious outlook on life and its relationship to healing was the bedrock of the message which he so powerfully exemplified in his life.

Part Two
Emmet Fox and Alcoholics Anonymous

The relationship between AA and Emmet Fox serves as an interesting and well-documented vignette in the early history of the fellowship.

When Bill W. and Dr. Bob began their work in the 1930s with recovering alcoholics, there was no AA literature. However, one of the very early recovering alcoholics who worked with Bill Wilson was Al Steckman, whose mother was Emmet Fox's secretary. Al was the first editor of the AA *Grapevine* and was responsible for coining the phrase "I am responsible" at an AA convention. When the early groups were meeting in New York, because of Steckman's connection with Fox through his mother, the groups would frequently adjourn after an AA meeting and go to Steinway Hall to listen to Fox, who would lecture to about five thousand people on New Thought principles.

Fox was an engineer by profession, raised in England, but the ideas concerning the power of the mind influenced him so profoundly that he dropped his profession and became one of the most popular lecturers in New York from the early 1930s to 1951.

An account set forth in *Dr. Bob and the Oldtimers,* a biography of the early AA history in the Midwest and specifically of the co-founder of AA, Dr. Bob, recites the influence of Emmet Fox and his classic *Sermon on the Mount*. One of the oldtimers in the AA program recited the following:

> The first thing he [Dr. Bob] did was to get Emmet Fox's *Sermon on the Mount*. . . . Once when I was working on a woman in Cleveland,

I called and asked him "what to do for someone who is going into DTs." He told me to give her the medication and he said, "When she comes out of it and she decides she wants to be a different woman, get her Drummond's *The Greatest Thing in the World.* Tell her to read it through every day for thirty days, and she'll be a different woman."

Well, I don't know if she was a different woman, but through the years I still read it and reread it. Those were the three main books at the time; that and *The Upper Room* and *The Sermon on the Mount.*

Perhaps Emmet Fox's fundamental contribution to AA was the simplicity and power of *The Sermon on the Mount*, as well as his other books that set forth in very simple language the truths of the New Thought philosophy:

> The usual metaphysical classes teach that God is the *only power, and that evil is insubstantial; that we form our destiny by our thoughts and our beliefs; that conditions do not matter when we pray;* that time and space and matter are human illusions; that there is a solution to every problem; that man is the child of God, and God is perfect good; that Jesus Christ is the one who taught the full truth about God, and actually demonstrated it.

Who could deny the power of Emmet Fox's language and its impact on all who heard it?

> Love is by far the most important thing of all. It is the Golden Gate of Paradise. Pray for the understanding of love, and meditate upon it daily. It casts out fear. It is the fulfilling of the

Law. It covers a multitude of sins. Love is absolutely invincible.

The statement of forgiveness made as part of the "pathway of love" set forth the program of fundamental transformation used by Fox:

> The Pathway of Love which is open to everyone in all circumstances, and upon which you may step at any moment—at this moment if you like—requires no formal introduction, has no entrance examination, and no conditions whatever. It calls for no expensive laboratory in which to work, because your own daily life and your ordinary daily surroundings are your laboratory. It needs no reference library, no professional training, no external apparatus of any kind. *All it does need is that you should begin steadfastly to expel from your mentality every thought of personal condemnation* [you may condemn a wrong action, but not the actor], of *resentment for old injuries, and of everything which is contrary to the law of Love. You must not allow yourself to hate—either person, or group, or nation, or anything whatever.*
>
> You must build up by faithful daily exercise the true Love-consciousness, and then all the rest of spiritual development will follow upon that. Love will heal you. Love will illumine you. Love will redeem you from sin, sickness, and death, and lead you into the promised land, the place that is altogether lovely.

One of the cornerstones of AA philosophy is to live one day at a time. Fox, throughout his ministry, emphasized that one of most important rules in metaphysics is to live in the present:

> Live in today, and do not allow yourself to live in the past under any pretense. Living in the past means thinking about the past, rehearsing past events, especially if you do this with feeling. . . . Train yourself to be a man or woman who lives one day at a time. You'll be surprised how rapidly conditions will change for the better when you approach this ideal.

From Fox's example may have developed AA's tradition of nonownership of property; Fox's ministry declined the ownership of property and the management of buildings and used hotel ballrooms and theaters for sermons and meetings. Fox himself supported and encouraged this practice.

> The great peril in true religion has always been the building up of vested interest in wealthy organizations, or in the exploitation by individuals or their own personality. When this happens, the rank and file are sure to be severely discouraged from seeking spiritual things for themselves at firsthand.

Fox's first sermons were given in the ballrooms of various small hotels, using loudspeakers. By 1936, the crowds had grown so that the Sunday services were moved to the Astor Hotel. For many years thereafter, Fox delivered three weekday lectures in addition to the regular one on Sunday morning. He spoke on Wednesday at noon at the Biltmore Hotel, on Friday at noon at the Astor, and on the next Wednesday at the Manhattan Opera House.

On March 14, 1937, the Church of the Healing Christ conducted a special service in the Hippodrome. It was so successful that the congregation met there regularly for the following month. Thereafter the group was moved to the larger Manhattan Opera House, and finally to the even larger Carnegie Hall. Usually Fox addressed five thousand to six thousand people on Wednesday evenings and Sunday mornings, and on special occasions the figure reached eight thousand.

From Emmet Fox's emphasis on the fact that thoughts are real things, and that one cannot have one kind of mind and another kind of life, came the pattern of changing based upon a new look on life. According to Fox, any thought pattern that is persisted in must sooner or later materialize in a person's outer circumstances. If you want to change your life, you must change your thoughts first.

AA used much of his simply stated profundities to create a philosophy that now transforms the lives of millions of recovering alcoholics. Five of the original stories in the Big Book were by early AA members deeply influenced by Emmet Fox. Truly, he was an inspirational figure in AA's early era.

Part Three

The Jack Alexander Article

Publication of "Alcoholics Anonymous," by Jack Alexander, in the *Saturday Evening Post* of March 1, 1941, marked a milestone in the history of AA.

Although one national article had been published before that date, the *Post* report on the first two thousand men and women who had achieved sobriety through AA was largely responsible for the surge of interest that established the fellowship on a national and international basis.

The article inspired a deluge of mail to the small New York office of AA, and the response soon overtaxed what co-founder Bill W. described at the time as "a recently enlarged staff, now four." Volunteer AAs and their wives were called in to help write personal replies to the forty-four hundred often-desperate inquiries that poured in over the next several months. Due to the *Post* article, AA membership tripled by the end of 1941. This increased the confidence of the small, uncertain AA groups then in existence. The prestige of the *Post* and the example it set encouraged many newspapers to inform their readers of this strange fellowship of former drunks who helped other alcoholics get and stay sober.

In 1941, more than half of AA's current members were teenagers, children—or not even born. Oldtimers and newcomers alike, virtually all AAs owe a debt of gratitude to Jack Alexander, who died in 1975. His talent, diligence, and insight focused the first strong favorable light on AA. Jack remained a lifelong friend of the fellowship, serving eventually as a nonalcoholic trustee on AA's General Service Board.

Following is the article as it appeared in 1941:

Three men sat around the bed of an alcoholic patient in the psychopathic ward of Philadelphia General Hospital one afternoon a few weeks ago. The man in the bed, who was a complete stranger to them, had the drawn and slightly stupid look that inebriates get while being defogged after a bender. The only thing that was noteworthy about the callers, except for the obvious contrast between their well-groomed appearances and that of the patient, was the fact that each had been through the defogging process many times himself. They were members of Alcoholics Anonymous, a band of ex-problem drinkers who made an avocation of helping other alcoholics to beat the liquor habit.

The man in the bed was a mechanic. His visitors had been educated at Princeton, Yale, and Pennsylvania and were, by occupation, a salesman, a lawyer, and a publicity man. Less than a year before, one had been in shackles in the same ward. One of his companions had been what is known among alcoholics as a sanitarium commuter. He had moved from place to place, bedeviling the staffs of the country's leading institutions for the treatment of alcoholics. The other had spent twenty years of life, all outside institution walls, making life miserable for himself and his family and his employers, as well as sundry well-meaning relatives who had had the temerity to intervene.

The air of the ward was thick with the aroma of paraldehyde, an unpleasant cocktail smelling like a mixture of alcohol and ether, which hospitals sometimes use to taper off the paralyzed drinker and soothe his squirming nerves. The visitors seemed oblivious of this and of the depressing atmosphere that clings to even the nicest of psychopathic wards. They smoked and talked with the patient for twenty minutes or so, then left their personal cards and departed. If the man in the bed felt that he would like to see one of them again, they told him, he had only to put in a telephone call.

They made it plain that if he actually wanted to stop drinking, they would leave their work or get up in the middle of the night to hurry to where he was. If he did not choose to call, that would be the end of it. The members of Alcoholics Anonymous do not pursue or coddle a malingering prospect, and they know the strange tricks of the alcoholic as a reformed swindler knows the art of bamboozling.

Herein lies much of the unique strength of a movement which, in the past six years, has brought recovery to around 2,000 men and women, a large percentage of whom had been considered medically hopeless. Doctors and clergymen, working separately or together, have always managed to salvage a few cases. In isolated instances, drinkers have found their own methods of quitting. But the inroads into alcoholism have been negligible, and it remains one of the great unsolved public-health enigmas.

By nature touchy and suspicious, the alcoholic likes to be left alone to work out his puzzle, and he has a convenient way of ignoring the tragedy which he inflicts meanwhile upon those who are close to him. He holds desperately to a conviction that, although he has not been able to handle alcohol in the past, he will ultimately succeed in becoming a controlled drinker. One of medicine's queerest animals, he is, often as not, an acutely intelligent person. He fences with professional men and relatives who attempt to aid him, and he gets a perverse satisfaction out of tripping them up in argument.

There is no specious excuse for drinking which the troubleshooters of Alcoholics Anonymous have not heard or used themselves. When one of their prospects hands them a rationalization for getting soused, they match it with half a dozen out of their own experiences. This upsets him a little, and he gets defensive. He looks at their neat clothing and smoothly shaved faces and charges them with being goody-goodies who don't know what it is to struggle with drink. They reply by relating their own stories: the double Scotches and brandies before breakfast; the vague feeling of discomfort which precedes a drinking bout; the awakening from a spree without being able to account for their actions of several days and the haunting fear that possibly they had run down someone with their automobiles.

They tell of the eight-ounce bottles of gin hidden behind pictures and in caches from cellar to attic; of spending whole days in motion-picture houses to stave off the temptation to drink; of sneaking out of the office for quickies during the day. They talk of losing jobs and stealing money from their wives' purses; of putting pepper into whiskey to give it a tang; of tippling on bitters and sedative tablets, or on mouthwash or hair tonic; of getting into the habit of camping outside the neighborhood tavern ten minutes before opening time. They describe a hand so jittery that it could not lift a pony to the lips without spilling the contents; drinking liquor from a beer stein because it can be steadied with two hands, although at the risk of chipping a front tooth; tying an end of a towel about a glass, looping the towel around the back of the neck, and drawing the free end with the other hand, pulley fashion, to advance the glass to the mouth; hands so shaky they feel as if they were about to snap off and fly into space; sitting on hands for hours to keep them from doing this.

These and other bits of drinking lore usually manage to convince the alcoholic that he is talking to blood brothers. A bridge of confidence is thereby erected, spanning a gap which has baffled the physician, the minister, the priest, or the hapless relatives. Over this connection, the troubleshooters convey, bit by bit, the details of a program for living which has worked for them and which, they feel, can work for any other alcoholic. They concede as out of their orbit only those who are psychotic or who are already suffering from the physical impairment known as wet brain. At the same time, they see to it that the prospect gets whatever medical attention is needed.

Many doctors and staffs of institutions throughout the country now suggest Alcoholics Anonymous to their drinking patients. In some towns, the courts and probation officers cooperate with the local group. In a few city psychopathic divisions, the workers of Alcoholics Anonymous are accorded the same visiting privileges as staff members. Philadelphia General is one of these. Dr. John F. Stouffer, the chief psychiatrist, says: "The alcoholics we get here are mostly those who cannot afford private treatment, and this is by far the greatest thing we have ever been able to offer them. Even among those who occasionally land back in here again, we observe a profound change in personality. You would hardly recognize them."

The *Illinois Medical Journal*, in an editorial last December, went further than Dr. Stouffer in stating: "It is indeed a miracle when a person who for years has been more or less constantly under the influence of alcohol and in whom his friends have lost all confidence, will sit up all night with a drunk and at stated intervals administer a small amount of liquor in accordance with a doctor's order without taking a drop himself."

This is a reference to a common aspect of the Arabian Nights adventures to which Alcoholics Anonymous workers dedicate themselves. Often it involves sitting upon, as well as up with, the intoxicated person, as the impulse to jump out a window seems to be an attractive one to many alcoholics when in their cups. Only an alcoholic can squat on another alcoholic's chest for hours with the proper combination of discipline and sympathy.

During a recent trip around the East and Middle West, I met and talked with scores of AAs, as they call themselves, and found them to be unusually calm, tolerant people. Somehow, they seemed better integrated than the average group of nonalcoholic individuals. Their transformation from cop fighters, canned-heat drinkers, and, in some instances, wife beaters, was startling. On one of the most influential newspapers in the country, I found that the city editor, the assistant city editor, and a nationally known reporter were AAs, and strong in the confidence of their publisher.

In another city, I heard a judge parole a drunken driver to an AA member. The latter, during his drinking days, had smashed several cars and had had his own operator's license suspended. The judge knew him and was glad to trust him. A brilliant executive of an advertising firm disclosed that two years ago he had been panhandling and sleeping in a doorway under an elevated structure. He had a favorite doorway, which he shared with other vagrants, and every few weeks he goes back and pays them a visit just to assure himself he isn't dreaming.

In Akron, as in other manufacturing centers, the groups include a heavy element of manual workers. In the Cleveland Athletic Club, I had luncheon with five lawyers, an accountant, an engineer, three salesmen, an insurance man, a buyer, a bartender, a chain-store manager, a manager of an independent store, and a manufacturer's representative. They were members of a central committee which coordinates the work of nine neighborhood groups. Cleveland, with more than 450 members, is the biggest of the AA centers. The next largest are located in Chicago, Akron, Philadelphia, Los Angeles, Washington, and New York. All told, there are groups in about fifty cities and towns.

In discussing their work, the AAs spoke of their drunk-rescuing as "insurance" for themselves. Experience within the group has shown, they said, that once a recovered drinker slows up in this work, he is likely to go back to drinking himself. There is, they agreed, no such thing as an ex-alcoholic. If one is an alcoholic—that is, a person who is unable to drink normally—one remains an alcoholic until he dies, just as a diabetic remains a diabetic. The best he can hope for is to become an arrested case, with drunk-saving as his insulin. At least, the AAs say so, and medical opinion tends to support them. All but a few said that they had lost all desire for alcohol. Most serve liquor in their homes when friends drop in, and they still go to bars with companions who drink. The AAs tipple on soft drinks and coffee.

One, a sales manager, acts as bartender at his company's annual jamboree in Atlantic City and spends his nights tucking the celebrators into their beds. Only a few of those who recover fail to lose the feeling that at any minute they may thoughtlessly take one drink and skyrocket off on a disastrous binge. An AA who is a clerk in an Eastern city hasn't had a snifter in three and a half years, but says that he still has to walk fast past saloons to circumvent the old impulse; but he is an exception. The only hangover from the wild days that plagues the AA is a recurrent nightmare. In the dream, he finds himself off on a rousing whooper-dooper, frantically trying to conceal his condition from the community. Even this symptom disappears shortly, in most cases. Surprisingly, the rate of employment among these people, who formerly drank themselves out of job after job, is said to be around 90 percent.

One-hundred-percent effectiveness with nonpsychotic drinkers who sincerely want to quit is claimed by the workers of Alcoholics Anonymous. The program will not work, they add, with those who only "want to want to quit," or who want to quit because they are afraid of losing their families or their jobs. The effective desire, they state, must be based upon enlightened self-interest; the applicant must want to get away from liquor to head off incarceration or premature death. He must be fed up with the stark social loneliness which engulfs the uncontrolled drinker, and he must want to put some order into his bungled life.

As it is impossible to disqualify all borderline applicants, the working percentage of recovery falls below the 100-percent mark. According to AA estimation, 50 percent of the alcoholics taken in hand recover almost immediately; 25 percent get well after suffering a relapse or two; and the rest remain doubtful. This rate of success is exceptionally high. Statistics on traditional medical and religious cures are lacking, but it has been informally estimated that they are no more than 2 or 3 percent effective on run-of-the-mill cases.

Although it is too early to state that Alcoholics Anonymous is the definitive answer to alcoholism, its brief record is impressive, and it is receiving hopeful support. John D. Rockefeller, Jr., helped defray the expense of getting it started and has gone out of his way to get other prominent men interested.

Rockefeller's fight was a small one, in deference to the insistence of the originators that the movement be kept on a voluntary, nonpaid basis. There are no salaried organizers, no dues, no officers, and no central control. Locally, the rents of assembly halls are met by passing the hat at meetings. In small communities, no collections are taken, as the gatherings are held in private homes. A small office in downtown New York acts merely as a clearinghouse for information. There is no name on the door, and mail is received anonymously through a post-office box. The only income, which is money received from the sale of a book describing the work, is handled by the Alcoholic Foundation, a board composed of three alcoholics and four nonalcoholics. . . .

Why some people become alcoholics is a question on which authorities disagree. Few think that anyone is "born an alcoholic." One may be born, they say, with a hereditary predisposition to alcoholism, just as one may be born with a vulnerability to tuberculosis. The rest seems to depend upon environment and experience, although one theory has it that some people are allergic to alcohol, as hayfever sufferers are to pollens. Only one note is found to be common to all alcoholics—emotional immaturity. Closely related to this is an observation that an unusually large number of alcoholics start out in life as an only child, as a younger child, as the only boy in a family of girls or the only girl in a family of boys. Many have records of childhood precocity and were what are known as spoiled children.

Frequently, the situation is complicated by an off-center home atmosphere in which one parent is unduly cruel, the other overindulgent. Any combination of these factors, plus a divorce or two, tends to produce neurotic children who are poorly equipped emotionally to face the ordinary realities of adult life. In seeking escapes, one may immerse himself in his business, working twelve to fifteen hours a day, or in sports, or in some artistic sideline. Another finds what he thinks is a pleasant escape in drink. It bolsters his opinion of himself and temporarily wipes away any feeling of social inferiority which he may have. Light drinking leads to heavy drinking. Friends and family are alienated and employers become disgusted. The drinker smolders with resentment and wallows in self-pity. He indulges in childish rationalizations to justify his drinking: he has been working hard, and he deserves to relax; his throat hurts from an old tonsillectomy and a drink would ease the pain; he has a headache; his wife does not understand him; his nerves are jumpy; everybody is against him; and so on and on. He unconsciously becomes a chronic excuse-maker for himself.

All the time he is drinking, he tells himself and those who butt in to his affairs that he can really become a controlled drinker if he wants to. To demonstrate his strength of will, he goes for weeks without taking a drop. He makes a point of calling on his favorite bar at a certain time each day and ostentatiously sipping milk or a carbonated beverage, not realizing that he is indulging in juvenile exhibitionism. Falsely encouraged, he shifts to a routine of one beer a day, and that is the beginning of the end once more. This leads inevitably to more beer and then to hard liquor. Hard liquor leads to another first-rate bender. Oddly, the trigger which sets off the explosion is as apt to be a stroke of business success as it is to be a run of bad luck. An alcoholic can stand neither prosperity nor adversity.

The victim is puzzled on coming out of the alcoholic fog. Without his being aware of any change, a habit has gradually become an obsession. After a while, he no longer needs rationalizations to justify the fatal first drink. All he knows is that he feels swamped by uneasiness, and before he realizes what is happening, he is standing at a bar with an empty whiskey pony in front of him and a stimulating sensation in his throat. By some peculiar quirk of his mind, he has been able to draw a curtain over the memory of the intense pain and remorse caused by preceding stem winders. After many experiences of this kind, the alcoholic begins to realize that he does not understand himself, he wonders whether his power of will, though strong in other fields, isn't defenseless against alcohol. He may go on trying to defeat his obsession and wind up in a sanitarium. He may give up the fight as hopeless and try to kill himself. Or he may seek outside help.

If he applies to Alcoholics Anonymous, he is first brought around to admit that alcohol has him whipped and that his life has become unmanageable. Having achieved this state of intellectual humility, he is given a dose of religion in its broadest sense. He is asked to believe in a Power that is greater than himself, or at least to keep an open mind on that subject while he goes on with the rest of the program. Any concept of the Higher Power is acceptable. A skeptic or agnostic may choose to think of his inner self, the miracle of growth, a tree, man's wonderment at the physical universe, the structure of the atom, or mere mathematical infinity. Whatever form is visualized, the neophyte is taught that he must rely upon it and, in his own way, pray to the Power for strength.

He next makes a sort of moral inventory of himself with the private aid of another person—one of his AA sponsors, a priest, a minister, a psychiatrist, or anyone else he fancies. If it gives him relief, he may get up at a meeting and recite his misdeeds, but he is not required to do so. He restores what he may have stolen while intoxicated and arranges to pay off old debts and to make good on rubber checks; he makes amends to persons he has abused and, in general, cleans up his past as well as he is able to. It is not uncommon for his sponsors to lend him money to help out in the early stages.

This catharsis is regarded as important because of the compulsion which a feeling of guilt exerts in the alcoholic obsession. As nothing tends to push an alcoholic toward the bottle more than personal resentments, the pupil also makes out a list of his grudges and resolves not to be stirred by them. At this point, he is ready to start working on other, active alcoholics. By the process of extroversion, which the work entails, he is able to think less of his own troubles.

The more drinkers he succeeds in swinging into Alcoholics Anonymous, the greater his responsibility to the group becomes. He can't get drunk now without injuring the people who have proved themselves his best friends. He is beginning to grow up emotionally and to quit being a leaner. If raised in an orthodox church, he usually, but not always, becomes a regular communicant again.

Simultaneously with the making over of the alcoholic goes the process of adjusting his family to his new way of living. The wife or husband of an alcoholic, and the children, too, frequently become neurotics from being exposed to drinking excesses over a period of years. Reeducation of the family is an essential part of a follow-up program which has been devised.

Alcoholics Anonymous, which is a synthesis of old ideas rather than a new discovery, owes its existence to the collaboration of a New York stockbroker and an Akron physician. Both alcoholics, they met for the first time a little less than six years ago. In thirty-five years of periodic drinking, Dr. Armstrong, to give the physician a fictitious name, had drunk himself out of most of his practice. Armstrong had tried everything, including the Oxford Group, and had shown no improvement. On Mother's Day, 1935, he staggered home, in typical drunk fashion, lugging an expensive potted plant, which he placed in his wife's lap. Then he went upstairs and passed out.

At that moment, nervously pacing the lobby of an Akron hotel was the broker from New York, whom we shall arbitrarily call Griffith. Griffith was in a jam. In an attempt to obtain control of a company and rebuild his financial fences, he had come out to Akron and engaged in a fight for proxies. He had lost the fight. His hotel bill was unpaid. He was almost flat broke. Griffith wanted a drink.

During his career in Wall Street, Griffith had turned some sizable deals and had prospered, but, through ill-timed drinking bouts, had lost out on his main chances. Five months before coming to Akron, he had gone on the water wagon through the ministrations of the Oxford Group in New York. Fascinated by the problem of alcoholism, he had many times gone back as a visitor to a Central Park West detoxicating hospital, where he had been a patient, and talked to the inmates. He effected no recoveries, but found that by working on other alcoholics he could stave off his own craving.

A stranger in Akron, Griffith knew no alcoholics with whom he could wrestle. A church directory which hung in the lobby opposite the bar gave him an idea. He telephoned one of the clergymen listed and through him got in touch with a member of the local Oxford Group. This person was a friend of Dr. Armstrong's and was able to introduce the physician and the broker at dinner. In this manner, Dr. Armstrong became Griffith's first real disciple. He was a shaky one at first. After a few weeks of abstinence, he went East to a medical convention and came home in a liquid state. Griffith, who had stayed in Akron to iron out some legal tangles arising from the proxy battle, talked him back to sobriety. That was on June 10, 1935. The nips the physician took from a bottle proffered by Griffith on that day were the last drinks he ever took.

Griffith's lawsuits dragged on, holding him over in Akron for six months. He moved his baggage to the Armstrong home, and together the pair struggled with other alcoholics. Before Griffith went back to New York, two more Akron converts had been obtained. Meanwhile, both Griffith and Dr. Armstrong had withdrawn from the Oxford Group, because they felt that its aggressive evangelism and some of its other methods were hindrances in working with alcoholics. They put their own technique on a strict take-it-or-leave-it basis and kept it there.

Progress was slow. After Griffith had returned East, Dr. Armstrong and his wife, a Wellesley graduate, converted their home into a free refuge for alcoholics and an experimental laboratory for the study of the guests' behavior. One of the guests, who, unknown to his hosts, was a manic depressive as well as an alcoholic, ran wild one night with a kitchen knife. He was overcome before he had stabbed anyone. After a year and a half, a total of ten persons had responded to the program and were abstaining. What was left of the family savings had gone into the work. The physician's new sobriety caused a revival in his practice, but not enough of one to carry the extra expense. The Armstrongs, nevertheless, carried on, on borrowed money. Griffith, who had a Spartan wife, too, turned his Brooklyn home into a duplicate of the Akron menage. Mrs. Griffith, a member of an old Brooklyn family, took a job in a department store and in her spare time played nurse to inebriates. The Griffiths also borrowed, and Griffith managed to make odd bits of money around the brokerage houses. By the spring of 1939, the Armstrongs and the Griffiths had between them cozened about one hundred alcoholics into sobriety.

In a book which they published at that time, the recovered drinkers described the cure program and related their personal stories. The title was *Alcoholics Anonymous*. It was adopted as a name for the movement itself, which up to then had none. As the book got into circulation, the movement spread rapidly.

Today [1941], Dr. Armstrong is still struggling to patch up his practice. The going is hard. He is in debt because of his contributions to the movement and the time he devotes gratis to alcoholics. Being a pivotal man in the group, he is unable to turn down the requests for help which flood his office.

Griffith is even deeper in the hole. For the past two years, he and his wife have had no home in the ordinary sense of the word. In a manner reminiscent of the primitive Christians, they have moved about, finding shelter in the homes of AA colleagues and sometimes wearing borrowed clothing.

Having got something started, both the prime movers want to retire to the fringe of their movement and spend more time getting back on their feet financially. They feel that the way the thing is set up, it is virtually self-operating and self-multiplying. Because of the absence of figureheads and the fact that there is no formal body of belief to promote, they have no fears that Alcoholics Anonymous will degenerate into a cult.

The self-starting nature of the movement is apparent from letters in the files of the New York office. Many persons have written in saying that they stopped drinking as soon as they read the book, and made their homes meeting places for small local chapters. Even a fairly large unit, in Little Rock, got started in this way. An Akron civil engineer and his wife, in gratitude for his cure four years ago, have been steadily taking alcoholics into their home. Out of thirty-five such wards, thirty-one have recovered.

Twenty pilgrims from Cleveland caught the idea in Akron and returned home to start a group of their own. From Cleveland, by various means, the movement has spread to Chicago, Detroit, St. Louis, Los Angeles, Indianapolis, Atlanta, San Francisco, Evansville, and other cities. An alcoholic Cleveland newspaperman with a surgically collapsed lung moved to Houston for his health. He got a job on a Houston paper and, through a series of articles which he wrote for it, started an AA unit which now has thirty-five members. One Houston member has moved to Miami and is now laboring to snare some of the more eminent winter-colony lushes. A Cleveland traveling salesman is responsible for starting small units in many different parts of the country. Fewer than half of the AA members have ever seen Griffith or Dr. Armstrong.

For (these) alcoholics, congenial company is now available wherever they happen to be. In the larger cities, AAs meet one another daily at lunch in favored restaurants. The Cleveland groups give big parties on New Year's and other holidays, at which gallons of coffee and soft drinks are consumed. Chicago holds open house on Friday, Saturday, and Sunday—alternately, on the North, West, and South Sides—so that no lonesome AA need revert to liquor over the weekend for lack of companionship. Some play cribbage or bridge, the winner of each hand contributing to a kitty for paying of entertainment expenses. The others listen to the radio, dance, eat, or just talk. All alcoholics, drunk or sober, like to gab. They are among the most society-loving people in the world, which may help to explain why they got to be alcoholics in the first place.

CONCLUSION

AA and Its Foundation: A Spiritual Awakening

One of the powerful and unequivocal promises made by Alcoholics Anonymous is that a spiritual awakening will occur when one follows fearlessly the Twelve Steps. Some individuals go to regular meetings in order to stay sober and go to step meetings in order to change from being victims to being responsible citizens.

The alcoholic is like an egg. He lives and moves within the shell of his own concepts; and within a certain area of the mind that is comfortable to him, he finds security. Within this area of the mind there are certain strata of thought-flow with which he becomes familiar—emotional stresses that he adjusted to as he matured. Within the eggshell he finds the pressures of his maturation pressing upon the boundaries of his accustomed area of mind and emotion. One day the shell breaks. When a person "hits his/her bottom," attends ninety meetings in ninety days, a rebirth process starts.

In this new area of an expanded consciousness, he feels the time of the "Pink Cloud." At this time the experimental teachings that have come down through AA are of value to him. These mystical teachings become the new circumference of mind, thought, and feeling in which he lives. After each new experience that he encounters, he turns toward the teachings of the slogans and the group sharings for confirmation, encouragement, and renewed understanding of sobriety. He unfolds naturally into a new philosophy, a new outlook on life, and seeks to put into practice all he has learned from within himself. To sharpen his sense of perception, he turns to the practices of the Twelve Steps and finds that his own individual will power plays a part in maturing and stabilizing the force fields around him. Previously, when he was unfolding inside the eggshell and experiencing the breaking of the eggshell, his individual will had no part to play. Now, as a more unfolded being, he discovers his inner will power; and, through the perspective of AA, he is able to use it to move his individual awareness into a greater enlightenment and this intensifies his life.

This then begins a series of inner experiences called, in the Twelfth Step, a "spiritual awakening," which becomes so vibrant and vital to him that he recognizes them even more strongly than the experiences of everyday life.

"We are condemned to live life forward, even though we can only view it backward," commented Soren Kierkegaard. Thus, the recovering alcoholic proves the validity of AA not by theories but by living in serenity and sobriety. An integral part of the program is its spiritual foundation; as Hugh Prather has said, "Alcoholics Anonymous is a Berlitz course in spirituality."

This spiritual awakening is available to everyone under all circumstances, and upon it any alcoholic may stop at any moment. It requires no formal introduction, has no entrance examination, and no conditions whatever. It calls for no expensive laboratory in which to work, because our own daily lives and surroundings are our laboratory. It needs no reference library, no professional training, no external apparatus of any kind. All it needs is that the alcoholic begins steadfastly to reject every thought of personal condemnation (you may condemn a wrong action, but not the actor), or resentment for old injuries, and of everything that is contrary to the Twelve Steps. He cannot allow himself to dwell on resentment of person, group, or nation, or anything whatever.

Central to the steps is the decision to surrender, embodied in Step Three, as the Big Book describes:

> We were now at Step Three. Many have said to our Maker, as we understood Him: "God, I offer myself to Thee—to build with me and to do with me as Thou wilt. Relieve me of the bondage of self, that I may better do Thy will. Take away my difficulties, that victory over them may bear witness to those I would help of Thy Power, Thy Love, and Thy way of Life. May I do Thy will always!" We thought well before taking this step, making sure we were ready; that we could at least abandon ourselves utterly to Him.
>
> We found it very desirable to take this spiritual step with an understanding person, such as our wife, best friend, or spiritual adviser. But it is better to meet God alone than with one who might misunderstand. The wording was, of course, quite optional so long as we expressed the idea, voicing it without reservation. This was only a beginning, though if honestly and humbly made, an effect, sometimes a very great one, was felt at once.

Through the Third Step, the recovering alcoholic builds up all the rest of the promise of AA, which will follow in a spirit of Love. Love will heal; love will comfort; love will guide; love will illumine; and love leads into the promised land of serenity.

Bill W. stated:

> Is sobriety all that we are to expect of a spiritual awakening? No, sobriety is only a bare

> beginning; it is only the first gift of the first awakening. If more gifts are to be received, our awakening has to go on. As it does go on, we find that bit by bit we can discard the old life—the one that did not work—for a new life that can and does work under any condition whatever.
>
> Do not let any prejudice you may have against spiritual terms deter you from honestly asking yourself what they might mean to you. . . . We are not saints. The point is that we are willing to grow along spiritual lines. The principles we have set down are guides to progress. We claim them spiritual progress rather than spiritual perfection. . . . We discovered the best possible source of emotional stability to be God Himself. We found that dependence upon His perfect justice, forgiveness, and love was healthy, and that it would work where nothing else would. . . . If we really depended on God, we couldn't very well play God to our fellows, nor would we feel the urge to rely wholly on human protection and care.

Exchanging amends is central to opening the Golden Gate of serenity. Making amends casts out fears, covers a multitude of sins, and is absolutely invincible. Amends are a kind of exchange. Like all expressions of love, which are miraculous in the true sense, the exchange reverses the physical laws, bringing love and peace both to the giver *and* the receiver. Amends undo the past in the present and thus release the future. Amends are the central growth device of the AA Steps, simultaneously increasing the strength of the giver and the receiver.

There is no difficulty that amends will not conquer; no door that amends will not open; no gulf that amends will not bridge; no wall that amends will not throw down; no "sin" that exchanging amends will not redeem, for amends allow one to recognize the illusion of what was perceived as "sin."

It makes no difference how deeply the trouble may be seated, how hopeless the outlook, how muddled the tangle, how great the mistake; the step of making amends will dissolve all pain. If you could internalize this concept, you would be the happiest and most powerful being in the world, for you would truly find the "peace which passeth all understanding."

You may say to yourself definitely, "My mind is made up; I have measured the undertaking; I have counted the cost; and I am resolved to attain the goal by the promises of AA. I can do this, and I will. Others may pursue knowledge to the farthest reaches of its wondrous growth; others again may organize great and marvelous enterprises for the benefit and uplifting of humanity; and still others may teach, and heal, and explore, or—if they feel the call—may scale the austere heights of asceticism; but I have chosen the path of the Twelve Steps of Alcoholics Anonymous. Henceforth, my field of work is right here in my own consciousness, and all my efforts and energies shall be directed to the cleansing and purifying of that from all that is not Love. Moment by moment, day by day, week by week, I shall root out from my own heart every atom of condemnation of my brother man, no matter who or where he may be, or what he may have done; every atom of resentment or any unkindness or injustice that has ever been shown to me, or to one that I love; every particle of jealousy of others, however cleverly it may disguise itself; every smallest thought or feeling, in short, which is not an expression of these Steps. My own heart is to be my workshop, my laboratory, my great enterprise and contribution to humanity."

This is the path of spiritual awakening promised by the Twelfth Step, and it requires no equipment beyond the readiness to practice it; no sacrifice beyond giving up the vice of victimitis, i.e., the buck stops with you. It is not only the simplest, it is the greatest of all the paths, great in the magnitude of its individual results, and great in the work it accomplishes for the whole race. To practice effectively these Steps is the quickest way to overcome all your difficulties, and because your mind is part of the whole of mankind, it is actually the quickest and most far-reaching way in which you can elevate all humanity.

It is the one path that is in practice open for everyone to enter, at any moment. Here the isolated student is at no disadvantage as compared with one who can command efficient teaching. Here the poor man has perfect equality with the millionaire, and the dull have exactly the same advantages as the intellectually brilliant. The plain man earning a modest living in the factory or store can practice these Steps among the surroundings in which he finds himself. The housekeeper at home, the sailor on the high seas, the farmer in his field, the nurse or the doctor in the ward, have all around them in their duties the perfect material for growth. The only question is whether one really is willing to pay the price—is really prepared "to surrender our lives and our will to the Higher Power." Chapter 5 of the Big Book makes it very clear that the only requirement is a rigorous honesty in practicing these Steps. The introduction to Chapter 5 says: "Rarely have we seen anyone fail . . ." except those who are not rigorously honest with themselves. As Dag Hammarskjold said: "The longest journey is the journey inwards."

About the Author

Igor I. Sikorsky, Jr., is an attorney who has been practicing in Connecticut since 1956. He was born in Stratford, son of the famous aviation engineer, Igor I. Sikorsky, who invented the helicopter. Igor attended Yale and Yale Law School. For several decades, he has been active in the civil rights movement and in the specialty that has come to be known as "wrongful discharge."